VALERIE BODDEN

grow with me

APPLE

CREATIVE PAPERBACKS

Published by Creative Paperbacks
P.O. Box 227, Mankato, Minnesota 56002
Creative Paperbacks is an imprint of
The Creative Company
www.thecreativecompany.us

Design by Ellen Huber
Production by Chelsey Luther
Art direction by Rita Marshall
Printed in the United States of America

Photographs by Alamy (Apex News and Pictures
Agency, Rusig, Thomas Weightman), Dreamstime
(Ivandzyuba, Ying Feng Johansson, Johnnydevil,
Robert Malo, Justin Skinner, Alexandr Vasilyev,
Vadym Zaitsev), Getty Images (Arpad Benedek,
Howard Rice, Wataru Yanagida), iStockphoto (artJazz,
Franz-W. Franzelin), Shutterstock (de2marco, Dhoxax,
Fotofermer, jocic, Ralf Kleemann, Irena Misevic, Maks
Narodenko, picturepartners, Olga Popova, Roman
Samokhin, Volosina), SuperStock (Animals Animals,
Biosphoto, Clover, PhotoAlto, Photononstop)

Library of Congress Cataloging-in-Publication Data
Bodden, Valerie.
Apple / Valerie Bodden.
p. cm. — (Grow with me)
Includes bibliographical references and index.
Summary: An exploration of the life cycle and life
span of apples, using up-close photographs and step-
by-step text to follow an apple's growth process from
seed to seedling to mature tree.

ISBN 978-1-60818-404-0 (hardcover)
ISBN 978-0-89812-990-8 (pbk)
1. Apples—Juvenile literature.
2. Apples—Life cycles—Juvenile literature. I. Title.
QK495.R78B64 2014
634'.11—dc23   2013029617

CCSS: RI.3.1, 2, 3, 4, 5, 6, 7, 8; RI.4.1, 2, 3, 4, 5, 7; RF.3.3, 4

First Edition
9 8 7 6 5 4 3 2 1

Apple trees are deciduous (*dih-SIJ-oo-us*) trees. Deciduous trees lose their leaves in the fall. Apple trees grow best where they have lots of sunlight. But they need cool temperatures in the winter, too.

4

Apple trees can be found on every continent except Antarctica. There are 25 apple tree **species**. Most of them are **wild** trees. Thousands of apple **varieties** grow on apple trees!

The leaves of deciduous trees turn colors and dry out in the fall.

5

6

An apple is ready to be picked when it separates easily from the tree.

The apple is a flowering tree that produces fruit. The seeds are found in the fruit. Apple fruit is often red and round. But some apple varieties are green or yellow.

Each apple can have up to 10 seeds inside it. A seed must be planted in soil to grow. Some seeds get planted when an apple falls to the ground and rots. Animals that eat apples leave seeds behind in their waste. People can plant apple seeds, too.

7

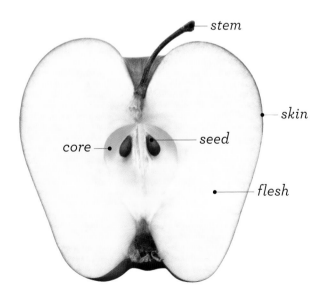

stem

skin

seed

core

flesh

Apple seeds grow inside parts called carpels near the core.

A seed is dry. Inside the seed is an **embryo** (*EM-bree-oh*). The embryo is wrapped in a hard shell called a seed coat. Moisture in the ground softens the seed coat over the winter. In the spring, the seed **germinates** (*JER-mih-nates*).

The embryo breaks through the seed coat. The seed's root grows down into the soil. Then a stem and leaves poke up through the ground. The new plant is called a seedling.

8

Wet, cool conditions help a seed sprout in two to three months.

9

10   *To help an apple tree grow straight and tall, it is strapped to a stake.*

An apple seedling's first leaves are called seed leaves. Apples have two seed leaves. These leaves store food for the seedling.

As the seedling grows, its stem becomes wider and stronger to form the tree's **trunk**. Branches begin to grow from the trunk. Leaves grow on the branches. The leaves use light, water, and air to make food for the tree. After two or three years, the seedling is a strong young tree. It is called a sapling.

11

Seed leaves are the first sign that a seed has germinated.

There is no way to know what apple variety a seed will produce. It will not make the same kind of apple as the apple from which it came. People can grow the kind of apple they want by **grafting** two trees together.

To graft two trees, an opening is cut into the bark of an apple tree seedling or sapling. This tree is called the rootstock. The rootstock will make up the roots and the lower trunk of the new tree. A bud from another apple tree is put in under the opening on the root-stock. The bud grows from the rootstock to become the new tree's trunk and branches.

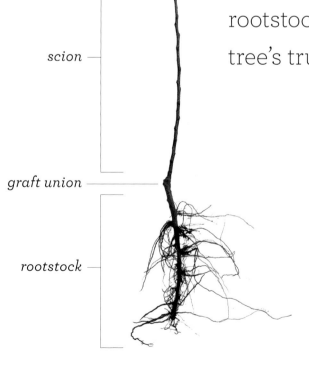

scion

graft union

rootstock

More than one type of apple can be grafted into a single tree.

13

14

The number of petals matches the number of carpels an apple will have.

The bulges at the tip of the stamens are called anthers.

When a tree's rootstock is 3 to 10 years old, the tree **blossoms** for the first time. In the spring or early summer, tiny **buds** cover the tree's branches. The buds open into pinkish-white flowers.

Each flower has five petals. The middle of the flower has thin **stamens** covered with **pollen**. The flower needs to be **pollinated** to grow into an apple.

15

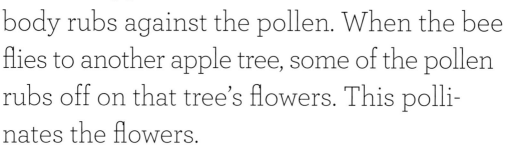

Apple trees cannot self-pollinate their flowers, so they need bees.

The flowers draw bees to the tree. A bee drinks **nectar** from an apple flower. Its body rubs against the pollen. When the bee flies to another apple tree, some of the pollen rubs off on that tree's flowers. This pollinates the flowers.

Pollen travels to a part of the flower called the ovary. This is where seeds are made. An apple flower can be pollinated only by pollen from a different tree. This is why people often plant apple trees in **orchards**.

16

American apple orchards cover 50 acres (20 ha) on average. 17

18 *About 2,500 apple varieties are grown in the United States.*

A flower's petals fall off a few days after pollination. The ovary starts to grow into an apple. Some of the apples will have only three or four seeds inside. That is because they did not get enough pollen. These apples fall off the tree.

The rest of the apples grow all summer. The tree's leaves make a special kind of sugar to feed the apples.

19

Apples are ready to eat once they are ripe on the tree.

The largest apple ever picked weighed three pounds (1.4 kg).

20 About 10 to 20 weeks after pollination, an apple becomes ripe. It fills with water and air. The fruit begins to make its own sugar.

Now the apple will taste sweet. It is ready to be picked! If the apple is not picked, it will fall to the ground during the autumn.

People can use apple pickers to reach fruit in the highest branches.

21

The covered buds are ready to survive the winter.

22 An apple tree loses its leaves every fall. The tree gets itself ready for the next spring. It grows leaf buds and flower buds. The buds are covered to keep them safe from freezing in the winter.

During the winter, the apple tree becomes **dormant**. Many orchard owners **prune** their apple trees during this time. Pruning will help next year's leaves get more sunlight.

Pruning can be done anytime but is most common in late winter.

23

24

After birds peck at the apples, the sweet smell attracts wasps.

People around the world eat apples. Apples make a healthy snack. They can be made into sauces, pies, juices, and cider, too.

Unfortunately, some types of pests also like to eat apples. Aphids are **insects** that feed on apples. So do some kinds of caterpillars. Many orchard owners spray their apple trees with chemicals to keep these pests from harming the fruit.

25

Thousands of years ago, people began to eat wild apples. The first **cultivated** apple trees were planted about 4,000 years ago in **Palestine**. After that, people planted apples in other parts of the world.

In the 1800s, a man named John Chapman traveled across much of the United States. He planted and sold apple seedlings wherever he went. People called him "Johnny Appleseed."

Johnny Appleseed

5

Johnny Appleseed was born in Leominster, Massachusetts.

27

5¢ UNITED STATES POSTAGE

28 *An apple tree will produce 7,500 to 12,000 apples in its lifetime.*

An apple tree can live 100 years or more. Each year, the tree goes through the same cycle. It grows leaves and flowers, is pollinated, and produces apples. And inside each of those apples are the seeds of a new apple tree.

29

Apples' outer coverings, or peels, contain healthy vitamins and fiber.

In the spring, an apple seed germinates.

The seedling grows and gains leaves.

In 2 to 3 years, the seedling becomes a sapling.

The seedling or sapling is used as rootstock.

After 3 to 10 years, the tree blossoms and is pollinated.

A few days later,  an apple begins to grow.

In 10 to 20 weeks, the apple ripens and is picked

The tree loses its leaves in the fall and becomes dormant.

After 100 years or more, the tree dies.

blossoms: *grows flowers*

buds: *small points on the branch of a tree that will grow into leaves or flowers*

cultivated: *planted by people, not wild*

dormant: *alive but not growing*

embryo: *the part of a seed that grows into a plant*

germinates: *starts to grow*

grafting: *joining parts of two trees together to form one new tree*

insects: *animals that have six legs and one or two pairs of wings*

nectar: *a sweet, sugary liquid that flowers make*

orchards: *places where many fruit trees are planted*

Palestine: *part of the Middle East, near the Mediterranean Sea*

pollen: *a yellow powder made by flowers that is used to fertilize other flowers*

pollinated: *is fertilized by the pollen of another flower, causing seeds to grow*

prune: *to cut off some of a tree's branches*

species: *groups of living things that are closely related*

stamens: *parts of a flower that produce pollen*

trunk: *the main, woody part of a tree from which branches grow*

varieties: *plants that have small differences from other plants of the same species*

wild: *living on its own, not grown by people*

31

WEBSITES

Crispy's Apple Stand
http://www.bestapples.com/kids/home.shtml
Check out apple facts, activities, and recipes.

Enchanted Learning: Johnny Appleseed
http://www.enchantedlearning.com/school/usa/people/ Appleseedindex.shtml
Learn more about Johnny Appleseed's work to grow apples in the U.S.

Note: Every effort has been made to ensure that the websites listed above are suitable for children, that they have educational value, and that they contain no inappropriate material. However, because of the nature of the Internet, it is impossible to guarantee that these sites will remain active indefinitely or that their contents will not be altered.

READ MORE

Llewellyn, Claire. *The Life of Plants*.
North Mankato, Minn.: Smart Apple Media, 2008.

Shofner, Shawndra. *Apples*.
Mankato, Minn.: Creative Education, 2002.

32

INDEX